I Wish That My Room Had A Floor

Living With An Emotional Disorder

By Rafael Woolf

With Mary C. Narducci and Phil Thomas

published by
VB Documentation Enterprises
Natick, Massachusetts

ISBN 0-9636942-4-3

Second Printing, October 1996, prepared by VB Documentation Enterprises, 60 North Main Street, Natick, MA 01760-3454

Original Publication, 1995, by Stone Soup Poetry, Cambridge, MA

"Social Worker Death Prayer" by Phil Thomas and "When You Were Little" by Mary Narducci were printed with the permission of the authors.

Cover by Victoria-Ann Bonanni was based upon an original illustration by Tamara Oraschewsky.

Printed by Eagle Graphics of Boston, MA

Dedication

To Virginia Candee, who poured so much love into me, and I never thanked her;
To Jere Abrams, who set me on the right path;
To Mary Narducci, for teaching me how to think;
To Lillian Pike Cain, Ph.D., my therapist, for helping me keep my feet on the ground.
To Marilyn and Phil Shapiro, Ellen Hertzmark and Shmuel Gedwiser, and Rabbis David Bachrach,
Shmuel Klatzkin and Gershon Gewirtz
for being friends in need;
To Center House and "Mass. Rehab" for the same reason;
And to Saint Francis House and the Samaritans
for showing people what we were put on earth for.
Also;
A special dedication to Phil Thomas for running himself ragged for the poor;
And thanks to my editor and publisher,
Victoria-Ann Bonanni of VB Documentation Enterprises.
Last,
A thank you to my mother.

Table of Contents

To Begin With

Explanations

Table of Contents (continued)

Progess

Friends

To Begin With

Preface

Mental and emotional illness twist the mind into shapes that are hard for the non-patient to understand. This book was written to facilitate that type of understanding.

Rafael Woolf
Brookline, Massachusetts
December 29, 1994

~1991~

A psychosis is just an exaggerated form of a disorder; a disorder is just an exaggerated form of a neurosis; and a neurosis is just an exaggerated form of what everyone goes through every day.

— Mary C. Narducci

You have to realize that the worst of all of this is separated from me by three different layers of confusion. I guess that's what makes it a disorder, the layers.

— Rafael Woolf

"Everything not forbidden is compulsory."

— used in The Sword in the Stone
by T.H. White

I feel bad, therefore I am bad.

Diagnosis: Generalized Anxiety Disorder

The Dome

When life somehow manages
To breach my defenses,
I am amazed,
Entranced,
Terrified,
Sometimes humbled
By what confronts me.

But sooner or later,
Whatever it is that impinged
On my consciousness
Gets digested,
Becomes a very part of the mind
It was once separate from,
Part of the very defenses
It momentarily conquered.

So I'm glad Life is real
And keeps getting through.

If not,
I would be—
    Suck as I might on my own self
    In search of the illusion of milk—
Very,
Very lonely.

The Abyss

If you want mankind's deepest fear,
Here it is,
Nothing else comes close:
Total helplessness, inside and out,

To be robbed of courage you so highly prize.
To be robbed of the inner peace
You hold dear as yourself.

To have NOTHING standing between you
And a world that's waiting to crush you.

In Judaism

In Judaism, there is actually some romance
In wrestling with your inner demons every day
(And taking a well-deserved rest on the Sabbath.)

If, that is,

If you're not convinced,
Deep in your heart,
That you're destined to lose.

Explanations

Hell

The world's my enemy; I am its
And mine.

There's no pleasure in my hatred.
Mine is not the comfort
Of feeling myself a private kingdom
Of royal contempt.
Here there is no compassion for myself, the hater.

I am in hell.

My sin is imperfection.

My soul perversely thirsts for this torture,
Rejects repentance,
Keeps away relief, shuts out love.

I can only sit
And wait until the strangely vindictive god inside
my head
Is satisfied I have been given my due.

Damnation

> "Depressed people never think anything's going to get better." — Mary Narducci

Damnation
Is the feeling
(Not the thought,
The feeling)
That nothing you do
Will ever measure up.

Damnation
Is the feeling
(The inner certainty)
That your lot is to be punished by the Universe
Again and Again.

It may only last minutes.
It can last a week.
It feels like forever.
Always.

Beware this feeling.
It can make you give up
On yourself
On others
Even on God
And court realer forms of hell.

Things Are Never Simple

Things are never simple
When you have an emotional illness.
A quarrel with a friend
Brings all sorts of half-related thoughts and feelings
To the surface:

Thoughts and feelings about your parents,
About policemen,
About bosses,
About lovers,
About the party you voted against,
And so on.

And all of them are clamoring for your attention
With equal force,
Great force.

Used to be,
All arguments were like that for me.

Getting Hung Up

Well, no, I don't wash my hands twenty-five times after touching a doorknob, and I don't feel I can't turn off the radio until it says something cheerful. But I can get hung up on details.

For instance:

The dryer has stopped. Will I feel more anxiety if I clean the lint screen before I take my clothes out or after?

It all depends on my conscience. My totally arbitrary conscience.

If its current obsession is cleanliness, then obviously, I will clean the lint screen first. But if its current obsession is that I obsess too much about cleanliness...and, by the way, whose fault is it, anyhow?...then I will clean the lint screen after.

If my conscience is bugging me about remembering the needs of others, I will clean the lint screen first. But if my conscience has decided, that day, that I worry too much about the needs of others (and, again, whose fault is it?), then I will save cleaning the lint screen for last.

I'm quite glad that the Still Small Voice isn't such a screamer.

Two Pieces

False Eternity

Like a dissonant high note
Held in an organ piece,
The anxiety of a disorder never ceases.
It gives a sameness to all days,
All seasons.
You are always waiting for the next...

Time

Panic attacks
Reduce time to only four:
Before, during, after...
And in between.

Fury A Clean Flame

There it is again.
That catch in my stomach,
<u>“Don't feel! Don't feel!”</u>
It traps impurities in my anger.
It forces it into perverse directions,
Including inwards.

Losing It

> "...what's at the bottom of all rage: fear. Violent, unmanageable fear." —Leo Rosten, Captain Newman, M.D.

Did you ever see The Boys In The Band?
It's a play about hostile gay people
And one who spends the entire second act
Taking his hostilities out on everyone,
Using alcohol—and his own self-hate—as fuel.

One night, in a fit of self-hate,
I yelled "nigger" in a poetry reading.
I have since tried to apologize
To every black person who was there.
I forgot why I was hating myself that night.
But I know what actually touched it off.
I tried to unzip my jacket,
And the zipper came apart.
And I was once more the little boy
Who broke everything he touched until
His father yelled at him,
"Put your goddam hands in your pockets,
Or you'll tear down the house, goddam you!"
I hate that little boy
And that he's a part of me.
I sometimes wish I could beat him over the head
With a shovel.

But when I hate myself,
I also hate everybody else.
It's one of my worst nightmares:
I've done something I hate myself for,
And I drive all my friends away.

So I feel and act hostile,
Until one hard-headed person
Overcomes my rage and panic
(Yes, panic),
And brings me down to earth.

Refined Paranoia

"The subway's stuck in the tunnel,
And I can't let myself get mad at the driver,
He didn't build it,
And I can't get mad at the Transit System,
Because most of their cars work,
And the occasional one that doesn't is the law of averages,
And I can't let myself get mad at the manufacturer
For the same reason,
And I can't let myself get mad at the car, itself,
Because that would be ridiculous,
And I hate being ridiculous,
But...

I happen to know
That every inanimate object that gives me trouble
Is always
Under the direct control

Of God."

Two Pieces

Compensation Neurosis

You've been nice and pleasant till it's got you in a funk,
So you feel you've earned the right to go beat up a drunk.

Short Memory

You're so proud of yourself when you're dong well
That you forget all the times you're a piece of hell.

Beliefs

The belief that it's abnormal to have a bad mood,
I have pretty much gotten rid of.

The belief that it's <u>sinful</u> to have a bad mood,
I have rejected intellectually;
But I have much more than intellect to deal with.

The belief that it's <u>dangerous</u>
Will take time
To uproot.

Uncovering Subliminal Thoughts

From a tenacious childhood belief
That it was sinful to have a bad mood,
It was only one short step to believing
That it was criminal for someone else to give me one.

That was my route to grouchiness!

Mood Taboos

The managing of my moods obeys taboos
Numerous and half-understood.
I must not get too happy
For too long.
I must leave some moods
Completely alone.
I must avoid anything
My mind labels as "risky"
(And the rules governing that
Are more changeable and bewildering
Than any others in my mind.)
Finally, there are moods I must destroy
To avoid disappointment,
Precipitous mood swings
Or the temptation of fate.

For Scott Ellis

And the world around me dissolved,
And I was standing on the prominence of a lonely bluff
With two stone giants,
One at either of my sides.

Stars above,
Stars below.

When a star came at me from above,
The stone giant at my left
Repulsed it with his mammoth club.

When a star came at me from below,
The stone giant at my right
Did the same.

And I knew these were my servants,
And I wondered why I had built them
And why I was so afraid of stars,
Although it seemed so logical,
Only because it had been happening
For so long.

When The Pain Begins to Stop

The Waning of a Disorder

There are more good days, now.

Days when I don't see significance in every detail
And a threat to my manhood in every significance.

Days when I don't have to keep active
Just to prove to myself that I exist.

Days without ideas sticking in my brain
Like cinders in my eye.

Days when I finally don't feel
That there's someone in my head
Pointing a loaded gun at me
And telling me to relax and be happy.

Spurious Virtues

Am I an exceptionally tolerant person
Or just a coward?
The more my nasty streak comes out in therapy,
The less my self-image is willing to look me in the eye.

Am I unusually perceptive
Or just cerebral?
The answer is yes to both.

Part of my progress is, beginning to prefer
Real virtues to exaggerated or spurious ones.
Still, I know, by the soft, spongy areas in my thinking,
That I have plenty of illusions, still, to lose.

Progress

My Therapist

I owe a debt of gratitude to whoever assigned me to Lillian Cain's group therapy. For years, she drove me up the wall with her insistence that I not analyze myself in the session (I do enough of that outside of it), that I only talk about what's happening in my life and how I'm handling it and how I could handle it better; by her prodding me to develop outside interests and get a job. I now know. She was making me develop a life that didn't have anything to do with my problems. Now that it's begun to work, I thank her.

It's Not Just An Insult, It's Also A Diagnosis

I'm a little obsessive,
A little depressive,
And quite a bit passive-aggressive.
It's a diagnosis as well as an insult.

And its' very unromantic.
I would do things sloppily,
Make stupid mistakes,
And kick myself each time—
Until I realized that kicking myself
Did nothing to improve things.
I would treat every mistake as a catastrophe—
Until I realized it was only making things worse.

I still act that way,
But not as much.
And being easy on myself was the key.
It was the only thing to do,
When being hard on myself only led
To repeated failure.

I knew I was making progress
When I caught myself being hard on myself—
Breaking the cardinal rule—
And thought,
"Oh, who cares?"

Two Sides of A Bogus Coin
The Sometime Stupidity

Well, how confused do you get
About good and evil and sex?

When I think of sex, the first thing that happens
Is my Inner Puritan tells me horror stories
Of people dragged by the Devil
Into a lifetime of sin and pain
And an afterlife of torture.
Then, my Inner Rebel retorts:
"Come on! It can't be that bad!"
(This, metaphorically speaking, is how I experience it.)
And meanwhile, neither mentions AIDS.

My Inner Puritan is fixated
On the dangers to my soul,
Period.
And my Inner Rebel's favorite fantasies
Are rose-colored ones,
In which my partner is always trustworthy,
And it is assumed that I've already asked her—
Without any embarrassment—
Who else she's had sex with,
And I never get carried away and find myself,
In the middle of the act,
Without a condom.

My inner conflicts about "good" and "evil"
Seem to end up leaving those realities
Out.

The Old Music

It's the same old
All-or-nothing thinking—
This time,
About anger.

My Inner Puritan (remember him?)
Says that if I even feel any,
I'm destined for Eternal Punishment.
(It knows how I hate punishment.)
Then, my Inner Rebel raises a hue and cry
And says that not only will I feel anger,
But I will bloody well express it
Whenever I want to.

And I sit in my Dome,
Watching things happen,
Looking for an opening
To insert some control.

The Buffer, The Bridge

I had an infatuation for the idea of a woman I know.

I knew the game from the beginning.
With no intention to let intimacy into my life
Until some really serious stuff is taken care of,
I love only by fantasy.
So I watched.
I watched my fantasies get born and grow
And wondered idly how they'd die,
What would destroy my illusions.

I liked her poetry.
I liked her body.
I liked that her heart seemed to have developed no schisms
with her mind.
I admired her from a distance.

And then, one night, purely by accident, I saw her scowl.
It had nothing to do with me.
She wasn't even looking straight at me.
But in my fantasies,
Which can think only in archetypes,
She went from woman, the lover
To woman, the monster.

That lasted five seconds.
Then, she was just another woman.

Fantasy is a buffer zone
Between ourselves and reality.
Fantasy is also a bridge
Between now and the future.
Some day, I'll have a tolerance for intimacy—
I don't have any, yet.
In the meantime, I go through regular rehearsals
In preparation.

Three Pieces

Wounding (1991)

Once,
A woman fell in love with me.
She was compassionate, intelligent, beautiful.
And if I had only known it, I was thinking inside:
"If this is what her good side is like,
Her bad side must be horrendous!"
I hurt her deeply,
And sadly, but firmly, she broke it off.
And I still curse the day I learned to distrust people
And believe only in unhappy endings
And werewolves.

Epilogue I (1994)

Once,
I joined a group of activists for the homeless.
They were softhearted, hard-headed, idealistic, realistic.
I caught myself thinking:
"It's all too good.
Somewhere inside, they must be hypocrites."
But I blessed the year I learned—
On a gut level—
Between the extreme best and worst expectations in my mind—
The existence of simple human decency.

Epilogue II (1994)

Once,
Recently,
I took a look at myself.
I saw my saintly expectations of myself on one hand,
My sometime, virulent misanthropy on the other,
And wondered what the hell normal was.

Untitled

When I was little, I curled up in midair
In an attempt to get to heaven.
Now, between here and the ground
Looks like an abyss.

Limerick (Traditional)

I wish that my room had a floor.
I don't mind not having a door,
But walking around
Without touching the ground
Is getting to be such a bore!

Agenda

I have a new agenda: when attacked,
To learn not to—in any way—
Side with the attackers.

I grew up with a dozen perverse ideas about love.
To love my enemies was imperative,
And loving my enemies was joined
To hating myself.
Where I got them, I don't know
Or care at this point
(Although it actually served me well, in a way,
Counterbalancing all my desires
To lash out at others.
Which came first, I wonder?)

I sit now in a restaurant,
Celebrating my new self-knowledge with an order of onion
        rings,
And take a leisurely examination
Of the fine points.
When will I stop seeing love as an attack?
Where did it come from?
Is it important to know?
My ongoing task, meanwhile,
Is always to learn
How better to love my friends.
It's the best long-term task
Of my life.

How Doctor Jekyll Could Have Done It Without Risk

He feared his anger and loathed his lust.
So be it.
He could have seen himself as their keeper—
Drilled a small peek-hole in each of their cells
And looked only as long—and as often—as he dared.

Then, when he was better acquainted with them,
And them with him and somewhat more tame,
He could have entered their chambers,
Gun in hand in case of emergency,
And simply kept them company,
Silently, if he wanted.

And as keeper and beast got used to each other,
They could have finally acknowledged
That they shared the same body,
The same person.

Eventually,
The cells would have become unnecessary.

October, 1994. The first set of layers is gone.

March, 1995. I've found my middle ground. It's not always solid, but it's there.

Friends

Realistically Speaking—

All right,
My fellow mental patients often get on my nerves.
Why should I say differently?
Some are the best friends I could ever ask for,
Some are the most fascinating conversationalists I could ever
        hope to meet,
And,
Some of them are boring,
Abrasive,
Rude,
Or give me the creeps.

What of it?

Would I vote them out of my community?
Not a chance.
No more than I'd vote out of my neighborhood
The rude,
Boring,
Or abrasive senior citizens
That also live here.

Any anyway, what would I use for a reason?
Mental anguish?

Medication

(for Diane Zagrodnik)

"Man,
They had me doped up!
In ninety percent of your mental hospitals,
The way they handle the inpatients
Is to keep them so tranquilized they can't cause trouble.
Or do anything else, for that matter!
So one day, they were handing out meds,
And I said, Uh-Uh.
I ain't gonna take this stuff.
And everyone around me applauded,
Including the staff.
You get that?
Including the staff.

So now I remember all the other doped up faces I used to see,
And some of them are probably still there.
And I wonder, man!
I just wonder."

Phil Thomas lives on the front lines of a helping profession. He knows what concrete anxieties are. I admire him, because most of his anxieties are for the sake of others...when he isn't afraid for his own safety.

Social Worker Death Prayer
by Phil Thomas

Those who go where murder looms
Helping people furnish rooms
Wear a curse born on the lips of
Theirs and thems race.
To ignore the pace of hate
Means breathing the fire of fate
Oh such an ungodly mistake
His and Hers trustworthy state.
When a deed means no coming back
From a vicious project attack
All the worms' eyes cast high.
Some people are good, but why?
Burros get laze in the sun
Knowledge knows that their porting ain't done
But social workers, the real ones,
(The ones who really bleed, real ones)
Move along in a fix
Hoping hard to avoid evil tricks...
And it's R.I.P. for the ones who
Didn't see complete the power of hate.

This poem, to quote its author, is about "that mode of thinking that the doctors call schizophrenia."

When You Were Little
by Mary Narducci

When you were little you played with toys made of the bones
and inner organs of small animals,
And Popeye's arms gesticulated among the patterns of the
paper on the walls of your bedroom.
Your secret friend, that nobody else could see, was
an animal named Glisher, and Glisher looked like a
skinned rabbit.
But you knew you must never tell Mummy and Daddy what
Glisher looked like,
Because that belonged among The Secrets.
Mummy and Daddy were always getting bigger or smaller,
so that sometimes you could hold them in your hand, but
mostly they huged over you and you were afraid you
would go back inside them again.
The only time they came on anything like their rightful size
was when they played their roles in the epic matinee serial
screened inside your head,
Stories stolen from funny books and radio,
And then their names were Wiggs and Oh Oh, the ineffectual
major domo and house-mother of a crew of murderous
Teddy Bears, pirates of shifting allegiance.
During the long boring years of grammar school there was
always between you and the world the screen of this
perpetual carnival.
So when the teachers, whose shapes were always shifting,
asked you questions, you never knew the answers, you
didn't even know the question
...Or only the raggedy end of it.
Dark sarcasm in the classroom translated into the feeding
frenzy of schoodyard bullying, because the other kids
needed someone to devour the way they were being
devoured by the bigger ones.

You got through it somehow, maybe because the voices of The
Gods, whispering in your ear or shouting from afar, were
more often right than wrong
When they told you what you were going to do a split second
before you did it.
Only a few times did this strategy of following their counsel
result in really disastrously inappropriate behavior.
But those were some of the worst times of your life, and the
Gods, abashed, would go away and leave you alone while
the jaws of the real world crunched you over.
It was a bright, passionate world, full of actions and artifacts,
a shifting mosaic like a computer animation. The grid was
always shifting,
Like images seen through water,
Like webs of light flashed from the waves upon the weathered
hulls of boats.
But when they made you take the purple pills,
All the bright actions and artifacts of your world looked like
they had been drawn by the drudges who illustrate
catalogues.

Mary Narducci, A Memoir

Mary Narducci retired from the alternative theater at an early age to make her living as a waitress and spend the rest of her time educating herself about the human mind. She had seen it in action a great deal. Her friends had been, and still are actors, musicians, and writers, many of whom had to take Haldol or Thorazine just to keep from flying to pieces. She is a devotee of Thomas Szasz and sees most diagnoses of mental illness as simply labels slapped on people by society to keep them under control.

Mary likes me, because I make good on my intentions. I never call her in the wee hours of the morning, unless it is a real emergency. I hang up if she is busy, tired, or in a bad mood and call someone else. That I <u>have</u> other people to call is a point in my favor. "Never," she says, "if you want the both of you to survive, put all your eggs in one basket. And if you don't <u>have</u> more than one basket, go out and <u>buy</u> some!"

One tidbit she dropped one afternoon was, "the connection between anxiety and inner ear dysfunction."

"What?" I asked.

"Fear o' losin' yo' balance, honky," she said in her way of switching from Oxford cadences to a Harlem drawl. (Her mother was black, and her father, Italian.)

I meant a lot to me. We all go through it, learning to walk, skate , or ride a two-wheeler. It's the in-between moment. You're not falling. You're not upright. You can go either way. <u>You don't know.</u> "It's the rapid pulse, the tight breathin', the tensing of the muscles." I picked up the ball.

"It's like the man who has to be in control. When events start getting away from him he gets anxieties, even though the turn of events could make him happier and richer."

"Uh huh," she replied, "and what about you? You're so afraid of your own feelings that any strong emotion feels to you like loss of control. And then you jump to the conclusion that it's pathological, that there's somethin' wrong with you, right? That's the medical model in action. O, the web we weave when we take our innocent children to the shrink! Oh, by the way, have you ever, ah, 'fallen' in love?" She shook her head solemnly. "It's <u>terrifyin'</u>!"

Systems Of Being American
You Don't Have To Have An Illness

Every time I'm under stress, I pop something sweet in my mouth.

I haven't got the faintest idea how to raise children, and I'm thinking of marrying someone who is into Zero Population Growth...but I feel guilty about it.

In fact, I feel guilty about a lot of things.

I'm afraid of love.

When I get upset, I...well...get upset.

I'm afraid of being hurt.

It took me forty years to stop blaming things on my parents.

I'm addicted to self-help books.

Every time I think about the hole in the ozone layer, violence in the streets, or the possibility of nuclear blackmail, I get nervous.

I have a craving to be perfect.

About The Author

Rafael Woolf has self-published many chapbooks of poetry and a one-act play, "Cain." From 1985-86, he was editor and publisher of the works of poet Bill Barnum. Two of his chapbooks have been published by others: Rent Free, written in collaboration with Phil Thomas and published by the Street Magazine Poetry Project, and this book, I Wish That My Room Had A Floor, originally published by Stone Soup Poetry and offered here in its second printing. Woolf has also contributed several articles to the "Street" and "Spare Change" magazines and has provided poems for many small-press anthologies.